Think Like A
MILLIONAIRE
Be A
MILLIONAIRE

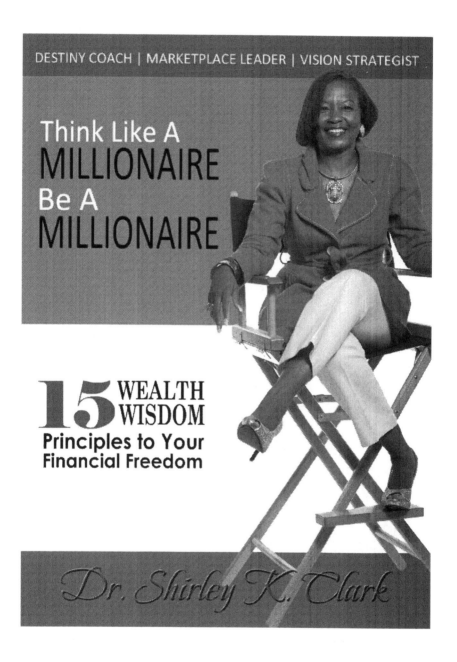

Unless otherwise indicated all scriptural quotations are taken from the King James Version of the Bible.

Think Like A Millionaire, Be A Millionaire
Copyright © 2015
Dr. Shirley K. Clark
Shirley Clark International Ministries

Printed in the United States of America

Library of Congress – Catalogued in Publication Data

ISBN 978-0692384046

Published by:
Jabez Books Writers' Agency
(A Division of Clark's Consultant Group)
www.clarksconsultantgroup.com

Jabez Books

Cover picture taken by Kauwuane Burton

1. Entrepreneurship 2. Personal Finance 3. Pursing Purpose

$\mathcal{D}$edication

This book is dedicated to Dr. Myles Munroe, his wife, and the seven others who died in a plane crash on November 9, 2014, while I was just beginning to write this book.

Dr. Myles Munroe was known for his incredible ability to exegete the scriptures, outstanding leadership, humanitarian kindness, and of course, his literary acumen.

Even though, I never attended his church in the Bahamas, I was one of his distant adherents. However, I, like many in the global community, have some of his books in my library. Reading his books or writings is like reading a scroll where every sentence is impactful. I remember the first time I read something that Dr. Munroe wrote. It was an endorsement for a book and it was exceptional. It was so well-written that it stimulated and provoked the writer to come out of me more profoundly.

His writing was so impressive that I began to study the anatomy of his writing. I began to study how he wrote it. How he formed the very essence of the story (endorsement) to make it say what it said. He was definitely an outstanding storyteller, scribe, pastor, leader and writer. The pen was truly his friend!

TABLE OF CONTENTS

WEALTH WISDOM #4

Man Was Designed For Accomplishment, Engineered For Success and Endowed With The Seeds Of Greatness.

-71-

-Zig Ziglar-

WEALTH WISDOM #5

Show Me Your Three
Closest Friends And I Will Show You Your Destiny

-83-

-The Late Bishop Mack Timberlake, Jr.-

WEALTH WISDOM #6

One isn't necessarily born
with courage, but one is born with
potential. Without courage, we cannot
practice any other virtue with consistency

-93-

-Maya Angelou-

WEALTH WISDOM #7

Success Has A System,
Manifestation Has A Method, and
Production Has A Process

- 103 -

- Yvette Munroe -

WEALTH WISDOM #8

You Cannot Expect
Victory And Plan For Defeat

- 115 -

- Joel Osteen -

WEALTH WISDOM #9

Wealth Is
Not For Self

- 129 -

- Dr. Larry Holley -

WEALTH WISDOM #10

Rich People Educate
Themselves, Poor People
Entertain Themselves

-139-

-Myron Golden-

WEALTH WISDOM #11

Dress The Way You
Want To Be Addressed

-155-

-Dr. Nassir Siddiki-

WEALTH WISDOM #12

When People Show
You Themselves, Believe Them.

-165-

-Oprah Winfrey-

WEALTH WISDOM #13
You Must Become The Architect Of Your Own Dream

-175-

-Anna McCoy-

WEALTH WISDOM #14
I've Never Had A Hater Who's Doing Better Than Me

-187-

-Bishop T. D. Jakes-

WEALTH WISDOM #15
Where Purpose Is Not Known, Abuse Is Inevitable

-205-

-Dr. Myles Munroe-

Definitions

-THINK-

Have a particular opinion, belief,
or idea about someone or something.
Believe, be of the opinion, be of the
view, be under the impression; direct
one's mind toward someone or
something; and use one's mind actively
to form connected ideas.

-BE-

Exist, occur, and take place.

Proverbs 23:7 says that as a man thinks, so is he.

Take-Away Conclusion:

If I think like a millionaire, according to the Bible, my life has no choice but to produce it.

Prologue

MILLIONAIRE IN THE MAKING

This book is a product of a temporary setback in my life that I was experiencing the week of November 3-7, 2014. It was an unfortunate situation that happened, and I told the attorney who was representing me in this matter, "Don't worry about it anymore, this is a spiritual war for me now." So I began to pray and ponder on the situation.

For the entire rest of the day and throughout the night I prayed and asked for guidance and wisdom as I worked in my office until it was time to go to bed. As I headed to bed, I felt impressed to pick up a book that was on my desk (that I just bought) to take it to bed and read it.

It was a book about success and money. I read about a fourth of the book, then I fell asleep. When I was waking up the next morning, I heard something like a title of a book - ***"Think like a Millionaire*."** Immediately, I knew in my spirit this was a book I was to write.

Afterward, I begin to hear regarding the content of the book. I heard that the book would be comprised of quotes of millionaires that are mentors and coaches in my life as well as quotes from a few other famous and rich people that impacted and spoke volumes into my life. Before I could walk to my office across the hallway, the book was solidified in my heart.

When I reached my desk and sat down, I got out a pen and a piece of paper and began to write the people's names down and the quotes that were associated with them that made an impact in my life. It was such an easy flow.

Even though I was dealing with a setback, I could still be fruitful in this season in my life. You see, no matter what negative season or circumstance you are going through, you cannot allow yourself to become barren. You have to persevere at all times to soar above these negative conditions that affect and/or threaten your purpose and destiny. So I refused to let this distraction going on in my life, define or cripple me from being **continually** fruitful.

My life is centered around me living in the overflow, not in some restricted non-producing environment. I **MUST BE FRUITFUL AT ALL TIMES!!!** So I was not going to let this negative situation have a space and time in my life that I would never get again. Setback, **I DON'T**

THINK SO. This was a set up. Now, I have legacy (this book) that will continue to bless people even after I expire. But even greater than this, a successful model for a new business was birthed in my spirit as well.

I saw the new business in its "wholistic" viewpoint with a lot of strategies for it to flourish and become a leading company in my industry. I was shown our uniqueness and the ability to attract customers. So much so that the calling of this great manifestation is pushing inside of me right now to get out. I am working day and night to take care of our current business-related tasks and clients, so my mental, physical and emotional energy will be focused on this new business opportunity.

Years ago I learned that the process of increase and acquiring wealth will always be met with conflicts. It is truly part of the equation. But noticed I said, "part," so it is not the "whole". Never mistake "**a**" component for the "whole". Never mistake a piece of the puzzle for the whole puzzle. Now, no doubt about it, the piece is important, but what we have to do is not allow the "deformity or impaired" segment of a thing to immobilize the entire vision. You may not control all the events and situations that happen to you, but you can decide not to be reduced to their level. You see, successful people see failures or obstacles as stepping stones to achieving what they want and unsuccessful people see them as personal and permanent obstructions.

Your innate survival navigational system knows the blueprint for success that is within you and how to bring it to fruition in your life. But just in case you are still stuck in a rut and you need a coach to help cheer you on – to tell you, you can make it; then this book is for you.

This book is a collection of quotes by millionaires that have impacted my life. Some of the millionaires you might know and some you might not know, but don't get hung up on whether or not you know them. Just be open to receive the message and the wisdom of each quote.

Many of us spend our lives listening to people who are not qualified to speak into our lives. This is the problem. When we are believing for increase and financial freedom, we must realize from the start that some of our associations will change in order for new relationships to be forged. This is so important because often our mindsets must be shifted by our encounters and associations for increase to manifest in our lives. Increase will always flourish in a ready and rich mind, a mind that the soil is prepared to receive the seed that will be planted in it.

I learned a long time ago that I don't know what I don't know. And if I would stay open for the new, no matter how much money my gift had brought me in the past, there is still another way that my life can be blessed by my gift. Truly, I am a millionaire in the making!

The day you decide to become wealthy and abundant, the universe will cheerfully provide.

--Mark Victor Hansen--

I remember the day I read this statement in Mark Victor Hansen's book, ***"One Minute Millionaire,"*** I felt as though a bomb had went off inside of me. I truly felt like an "enlightened" millionaire as Mark talks about in his book that we all need to become. ***The day "I" decide*** to become a millionaire, he said, the universe will come in alignment. I don't know about you, but this is an incredible revelation.

Often many think becoming rich has more to do with their education and what side of the "track" they matriculated from, but Mark Hansen's statement nullifies this thinking. It gives every man, woman, boy and girl permission to become wealthy, and I welcomed this permission when I read it.

After reading this section in the book, I put signs up all over my house saying, **"I Am Becoming A Millionaire."** I wanted to activate this statement immediately in my life. I also put signs in my children's bathroom that said, **"Mama Is Becoming A Millionaire."** I instructed them that whenever they go into their bathroom, they were to confess this. I put my whole house "under arrest" per se. I wanted my entire house to come in agreement, so the universe can make this happen *as soon as possible*. I wanted the universe to have complete permission to work on my behalf in my home and every aspect of my life.

Now I know for some of you this might sound foolish. But for those of you that come from the faith-based community, you should know that the Bible says, we can have what we say (if it lines up with the Word of God), and that the just shall live by faith. The reality is that for four years, I confessed this and believed it. Today, my income has increased three times, and continues to increase. No, I am not a millionaire yet, but I am on the right road.

You see, we have to start somewhere. And there is no better place to start or time to start than the present. The sooner you begin to activate what Mark said, the sooner your situation will change.

When I read this statement in Mark's book, I believed it, activated it and my situation did change. What caused this changed in my life? Three things.

1. <u>My understanding of how people become millionaires was altered.</u>

When we have little or limited information about money, wealth and success, it often takes us longer to acquire the level of financial freedom we desire.

My understanding or my concept of people becoming a millionaire was limited until I read this statement in Mark's book. The information I knew about how people got rich was good, but it did not have this understanding that Mark pointed out. Since reading this statement, I realized that having a limited understanding of how a person becomes wealthy was not just isolated to me. It was an overall pervasive problem in society I discovered as I talked to others.

When we have little or limited information about money, wealth and success, it often takes us longer to acquire the level of financial freedom we desire. Knowledge is truly powerful! All too often we talk about the world changing, but, we, many times need to do the changing. If we want the full effect, momentum or acceleration of reaching a certain goal in life, then we must have **all** the information for us to have agility in the process.

If a bodybuilder did not have all the weights he needed to workout, there would be a deficiency in being properly trained for competitions. And even though he would lift weights, his limited training could very well forfeit him the championship. This truth is the same in every aspect of our lives, and I might dare say, especially when we talk about money. We have to strengthen our relationship about and with money. We have to change some of our mindsets about money as well as respect money. Money begets money. I tell people all the time that many of the things we think rich people buy with their money is not true. A lot of things are given to rich people that poor people pay for.

2. I activated what I read

Google is my best friend and comrade in life. If I want to know something that I don't know or am struggling with, I Google it. But just acquiring the information I needed did not solve my problems. I had to do something with the information I learned. I call it being in an activation and manifestation stage.

Some things will only work for you when you work it. When I acquire information about something I need to know, I move into activation mode immediately. By me activating what I just learned, it causes my brain to remember the action or information more quickly. This is what you have to do when you get information about something or a subject matter; you got to activate it. This will cause the information to become a part of your life and to embed in your psyche quicker, facilitating a behavior modification.

3. I prayed and meditated

One of my greatest joys in life is basking and meditating in the presence of soothing music in the presence of the Lord. I constantly listen to music that soothes my spirit and keeps me in a state of tranquility. It is extremely important to me that I guard what I hear, see and think. While most people are going through crises about what is going on in the economy and the world, I decided years ago not to participate in it. Of course, I cannot alleviate all bad news, but I can limit the amount of negative information that comes into my hearing. I have lived long enough to know if I miss "this" crisis, there will be another one.

In the book, **"Who Switched Off My Brain,"** by Dr. Caroline Leaf, she said, "Every time you have a thought, it is actually changing your brain and your body – *for better or worse.*" She goes on to say that as we change our thinking, some branches go away and some new ones are formed, and the strength of the connections change and the memories network with other thoughts also. Therefore, as we think, our thoughts are activated and when they are activated, they activate our attitude, which will eventually reflect our state of mind." We are the sum total of our thoughts.

Furthermore, if we have a positive attitude, a secretion of the correct amount of chemical is released, but if we have a negative attitude, it will distort the chemical secretions in a way that it will disrupt their natural flow.

Your success in life depends on you focusing on the right things in life; thinking correct thoughts, and mastering the amount of space we give to negativity in our minds. When we do this, the universe (God) will give us what we have generated. True success is measured by the size of your thinking. **So think BIG!!!**

You can win success by believing you can succeed! Belief in success is the driving force behind every successful person, business, entrepreneur or organization. But just like belief will cause success in your life, disbelief will cause failure in your life. You have to observe your thoughts and only entertain those that empower you. Bottom line - think doubt, you will fail. Think success, you will succeed.

I was reading a book recently about the concept of belief and disbelief. It said there were three ways to debunk disbelief in your life in order to empower your believing. It said, number one, you have to think success and not failure. This is what I just said.

When faced with a difficult or challenging situation, think success instead of failure. Therefore, your mind (brain) will begin to generate solutions for you to solve the problem.

Second, remind yourself constantly that you are better and bigger than your thoughts. The key here is to understand that your current understanding has a limited understanding, and there is always something you don't know. Successful people are not superheroes. They are just ordinary people that made a choice to do something that others would not do. Always remember, the thinking that directs your intelligence is more important than how much intelligence you have. What are you after? You are after making history, instead of recording history with your mind.

Lastly, believe BIG. ***The size of your success is determined by the size of your belief.*** How bad do you want change? What would you do differently this year to make your dream come to pass?

For some, you might want to reduce the amount of hours you watch television or play video games in a week. Others might want to commit to reading a book on personal finance every month. And some might want to exercise more. Whatever you choose to do, **DO IT.**

In 2013, I wrote a book called, **"Pray & Grow Richer."** It is a book about how I was frustrated with my family financial situation, and I wanted to see a major change. From what I could see we were just living from paycheck to paycheck. Now, don't get me wrong, we were not broke, but how many times have you heard that it is not what you make, but it is what you do with what you make. Well, we were like this.

But if you looked at our finances, we would probably be considered a middle class family.

But let me clarify what this really means. Most middle class families have a lot of consumer debt, which we had years before, about $80,000. Thank God, we were able to get from under all of this years ago.

Also, it means they have a car note of about $15,000 and up, usually financed over a five year period for around $500 a month. Yes, we did.

As well, this means, they have a house note, which normally they pay anything from $1,100 to $1,500 a month. Yes, we had this, too. This list can go on and on.

But here's what I know now about striving to achieve middle class status or above. The so called middle class "American Dream" is really an "American nightmare," just like it was for my family. When we had all of that consumer debt hanging over our head, I did not know how to get out of our situation, but I knew we (I) had to do something different. So one of the things I decided I wanted to do was be mentored by millionaires consistently over a period of time. I wanted to acquire the wisdom of the wealthy, in the hope that I would learn something that would change my life cycle. I **ONLY** wanted to be coached by people who had made it, people who were extremely wealthy.

As I thought about how I could get wealthy people to mentor me, it looked pretty bleak since most of the wealthy people I knew were extremely busy. Then the thought "hit me," there are a lot of wealthy people who have already written books on how they made it and how we can do the same.

I hurriedly searched Google for a list of books to read, so I could buy them. I formulated my list. Then another thought came to my mind that reminded me that I probably did not need to buy all these books. I could find many of them in the library. To my delight, I did.

I checked out every book that was on my list and found some additional books to check out. I was a happy woman leaving the library. I can't tell you

There is a different impartation of wealth that comes on your life as you read books by wealthy people versus reading books by people who are not wealthy.

how empowered I felt knowing that my financial situation was getting ready to shift. I was confident about this.

And let me say this here, which is a critical point to you receiving the impartation of wealth upon your life from the tools you read. I **ONLY** read books by people who were actually millionaires. Not just people who were writing about the economy or business world.

You see, there is a different impartation of wealth that comes on your life as you read books by wealthy people versus reading books by people who are not wealthy, but just writing about wealth. There is a difference in head knowledge versus experience. What I wanted in my life was the experience to be manifested in my life. I didn't just want head knowledge, but I wanted the spirit of wealth to be activated in my life.

For four years, I stayed on this course. I read, prayed, soaked and meditated, and by the fourth year, my income increased three times.

Now, I am teaching others to do what I did. First, I wrote the book. Next I wrote a companion devotional journal, ***Pray & Grow Richer: 31 Days of Financial Empowerment,*** and then I was led to offer a free 90 Day Financial Empowerment Challenge. This Challenge was designed from some of the materials I got from some of the millionaires that I read about, plus some of the strategies I did to catapult or speed up my success matrix.

This Challenge is so easy, however, it requires perseverance, endurance and discipline to complete it. Most people start the Challenge, but over 50% of the people drop out after the first 30 days.

Stickability is the key to the Challenge working in your life. Most people have great potential, but it is not about ability, as much as it is about stickability. How committed are you?

One of the big reasons I offered this 90 Day Challenge is because one of millionaires promised that something significant would change in my financial or life situation if I used one of the exercises. **I believed it. I did it, and it worked for me.**

However, most people are not committed to their change. But for those who are, they will reap a harvest. Here are some testimonies:

- One man in 24 hours got a new truck for his business that previously he was leasing for $2,400 a month.

- Another woman got out of debt. This woman had never saved any money in her life. Not only did she get out of debt, she was able to save $3,000 in a matter of a few months.

- Another woman had a school loan of $12,000 cancelled while going through the Challenge.

- Another person wrote a book.

- As well another woman produced a CD.

- But the biggest testimony I heard was from a woman in North Carolina. She said she not only did the Challenge, but she read every book inside of my book that I recommended everyone to read. She said she did everything I told her to do daily. She said she had nothing to lose. And because of her commitment to change, she bought a new house with no money down. A new car with no money down. Then she received a check for $7,000, $3,000 and $4,000. So when she bought her home, she paid cash for everything in her house. Now, she is believing to pay her car and mortgage off by using the same principles.

You see, you can't tell these people it won't work. They have the testimony! And you can't tell me that it won't work. I, also, have the testimony.

YOU HAVE TO BE COMMITTED TO YOUR CHANGE!

There is so much more I can share about this, so if you want to know more about our 90 Day Financial Empowerment Challenge, email me at: Shirley@DrShirleyClark.org or visit my website at www.prayandgrowricher.com.

Wealth Nugget From This Chapter

True success

is measured by the size

of your thinking.

So think Big!!!

Recommended Books to Read

One Minute Millionaire by Mark Victor Hansen

The Next Millionaire by Paul Zane Pilzer

We Must Give Ourselves Permission to Fail and Permission to Excel

--John Maxwell--

The road to success is often laced with all types of soil and surfaces (dirt, gravel, rocky, paved, etc.). I am sure every successful person will tell you that this is a part of the journey.

It is said that Warren Buffet, the second richest man in the world, would never invest in any business where the owner has not fail at least twice. You see, each time we fail, we have a clue to our future success. John

Maxwell hit a home run when he wrote the book, **"Failing Forward."** It is a book that teaches us how to maximize every failure in our lives by making them learning opportunities.

I have a friend who is an attorney, who passed the bar after three attempts. Today, he and his family have taken over his family business and are doing quite well. And because of his law degree, it positioned him to run their family business in a spirit of excellence. He could have quit after the second try, but he did not. He could have felt like a failure, but he did not. When I sat down and talked with him about this ordeal, I was amazed with his candidness.

He said the first time he took the state bar exam, yes, he was disappointed that he did not pass. But when he assessed everything, he realized it was his fault. He said days before the exam, he and two other aspiring

No matter how incarcerated we might feel because of a setback, we can be loosed from our bondages and our gilded cages of failure to soar again.

attorneys checked into a hotel to study, but they did more partying than studying.

The second time around, he learned from his mistake, and studied like crazy, but he still did not pass the bar. However, he was determined not to let this setback stand in the way of passing the bar. So he tried it again. It is not how many times you fail; it's the lesson you learn to get back on your feet.

In one of my previous books on destiny and purpose, I quoted a segment from John Maxwell's book, **"Failing Forward"** that I believe warrants repeating here. He called this segment the "Rules of Being Human."

- **Rule #1:** You will learn lessons.

- **Rule #2:** There are no mistakes – only lessons.

- **Rule #3:** A lesson is repeated until it is learned.

- **Rule #4:** If you don't learn the easy lessons, they get harder.

- **Rule #5:** You'll know you've learned a lesson when your actions change.

Right now you need to assess where you are in life and see where you are based on these rules. For quite a few of us, I am sure, we will find ourselves in rule #3 – repeating the same lesson over and over again. Let's move beyond these barriers and get back on track. There is a chapter in the Bible that I love in the book of Psalm – Psalm 126.

It says:

> *[1]When the LORD turned again the captivity of Zion, we were like them that dream.*
>
> *[2] Then was our mouth filled with laughter, and our tongue with singing: then said they among the heathen, The LORD hath done great things for them.*
>
> *[3] The LORD hath done great things for us; whereof we are glad.*
>
> *[4] Turn again our captivity, O LORD, as the streams in the south.*
>
> *[5] They that sow in tears shall reap in joy.*
>
> *[6] He that goeth forth and weepeth, bearing precious seed, shall doubtless come again with rejoicing, bringing his sheaves with him.*

This Psalm is such a blessing to me. It is a Psalm of hope and encouragement. It says when the Lord turned again the captivity of Zion, **we were like them that dream.**

So often when we fail at something, it can be such a blow in our lives that our dream dies inside of us. But this scripture says that God can turn a bad situation around causing us to dream again. And no matter how incarcerated we might feel because of a setback, we can be loosed from our bondages and our gilded cages of failure to soar again. We can live again. We can dream again. I don't know about you, but this gives me incredible hope. My disappointments, my setbacks can be setups for me to dream again.

And this chapter goes on to say that your mouth will be filled with laughter and that the Lord is going to do great things for you. Wow, this is such an encouragement, and if we believe it, our success is inevitable -- we will win in the end – *"He that goeth forth and weepeth, bearing precious seed,* **shall doubtless come again with rejoicing, bringing his sheaves with him."**

Failure is a part of the process, but it is not the end **PRODUCT.**

Give yourself permission to fail and to excel!

Failing never makes you a failure, never trying again does!

*Each time we
fail, we have a clue to our
future success.*

Recommended Books To Read

Failing Forward by John Maxwell

The Confident Solution by Keith Johnson

We

Teach People How To

Treat Us

--Dr. Phil McGraw--

You will never change what you tolerate. This is such a true statement. In fact, today, I live my life by this philosophy. I believe if I don't tell or show people what I expect out of them in regards to my life, they will always mistreat or abuse certain aspects of it. Therefore, I am getting more and more assertive in letting people know my boundaries and how I expect them to respond and to respect my boundaries as well as treat me.

Don't get me wrong, I have not always been this assertive. But I have lived long enough now to know that what Dr. Phil McGraw said is true. Truly, what you tolerate is what others will do to you.

The way I learned this was in our business. We have a self-publishing book printing service, and for years, our prices were extremely low. However, when we worked with certain clients, they behaved as though they were paying an exorbitant fee. I don't know if you know about the publishing industry, but trying to edit manuscripts for first time writers can be quite challenging. It can be an extensive process. Many of the customers I was serving I knew personally, and over the years working with *some* of them became frustrating.

But before you get upset with my friends, let me say, I created this situation. I wanted each of my friends blessed so much that I started encouraging all of them to write a book. When they did, some of the manuscripts lacked content and good writing skills. So what did I do? Instead of just editing their manuscripts, I found myself writing much of the content for them, doing whatever it took to publish their books. However, I was only charging them a nominal fee, so my income was a "joke." Even though most of them had made a small financial investment, when compared to the service I provided, some of them acted like they were paying thousands of dollars.

When I set my standards at a higher level, I attracted the right clients – clients with a higher level of thinking.

Some of my personal relationships became strained as a result. Then finally one day I decided to make a change. I made up my mind that I was only going to work with business-minded people. I would only take clients who could pay my fees. I increased my fees to the right amount for the services we were provided, so I would no longer feel raped or undervalued. Guess what happened? When I set my standards at a higher level, I attracted the right clients – clients with a higher level of thinking.

The first client was a former news reporter from a prominent television station. She didn't shudder at the fact that the service she wanted started at $1,100. Then another person signed a promotional contract with us. She had an organization in downtown Dallas, where she owned an entire block. Needless to say, I learned a principle. I learned the principle of this chapter – *we tell people how to treat us.* From that day and until now, my income has increased every year.

How are you telling people to treat you? If people or your family are mistreating you, you are telling them to treat you like this. Because the day you decide not to take it anymore, this is the day your life will shift. Remember, you will never change what you tolerate! What most people do is try to wait for the other person to change before they change or before they make a decision. But this is the wrong formula. You have to tell people how you want to be treated.

Now, this does not have to be verbalized all the time, it can be communicated by your actions. You do something long enough, eventually, those around you will get the message. But even if they don't, you have clarified your position or boundaries, so for the most part, they know where you stand. Now, what you have to do is stay consistent. Of course, there may be a few times you might want to make some exceptions, but make sure all parties involved understand that this is an exception. Therefore, you have the right to change your mind. What you are doing is providing everyone with the information that they need to be successful in interacting with you in a particular situation or circumstance.

You have to create the world you want, and only allow people into your world when you want to. People should be privileged to come into your world. Never,

ever allow anyone to create your world for you because they will always create it too small!!!

You will never change what you tolerate.

Recommended Books to Read

Self Matters by Dr. Phil McGraw

Discovering Your Destiny by Dr. Shirley K. Clark

Man

Was Designed For

Accomplishment, Engineered

For Success and Endowed

With The Seeds Of

Greatness.

--Zig Ziglar--

When we were born, we were born with the potential to do great things inside of us. It is what we do with this potential that determines how successful we are in life.

It is said that the difference between average people and achieving people is their perception of and their response to failure. We have already dealt with success and failure in a previous section, so we are not going to focus on this aspect again, but rather, we are going to examine the concept of this statement from a different angle.

When Zig Ziglar says, "Man was designed for accomplishment, engineered for success and endowed with the seeds of greatness," I believe he understood the **need** for everyone to live up to their potential. He knew that there was an untapped reservoir in man, and if that dam was ever broken, it would release an overflow of blessings.

However, our ability to do great things lies within our ability to be diligent. Diligence is the gateway to keeping our focus. We have to do what others will not do. Proverbs 10:4 in the Bible says, *"The hand of the diligent makes rich."* It is what we do with "time" that determines our outcome.

If you are lazy and lethargic never working toward your passion in life, then don't expect greatness to come out of your life. I heard author, Scot Anderson, say it this way in his book on finance. "The Bible says that God will bless whatever we put our hands to. The problem is most of us are only putting our hands on our remote control." We all are endowed with seeds of greatness, but it is what we do with these seeds that defines our outcome.

I heard years ago that every child is born with every language inside of them to speak. But if a child grows up and have not learned or cultivated a certain language, their brain will decipher it out, making it harder to develop or learn in the future. But if the child was taught a language when he or she was younger, he or she would be fluent in that particular language.

This is the same with the seeds of greatness within us. We all have the potential in life to succeed, but we have to be committed to the task. "What we hope ever to do with ease, we must first learn to do with diligence" — Samuel Johnson, *The Life Of Samuel Johnson, Vol. 4.*

Diligence truly is the mother of good fortune. There is no substitute for hard work. Today, you have to make a decision whether you are going to go to your grave with the music inside of you or are you going to leave this world empty?

Also, you have to make a decision whether you are going to be an employer or employee. Employees are people who want everything given to them. But as a business owner or entrepreneur, you have to supply everything yourself. You have to create windows of opportunities and/or set up accounts with vendors that can service your business. A lot of time this is where the "rubber meets the road" in regards to people being successful.

I hear it all the time in the self-publishing book industry. I have people almost every year that call my office interested in publishing a book and becoming a best-selling author, but they do not want to go out and speak, do book signings, or offer any type of special training to promote their book. I have to let them know if they want their book to sell, they have to create an interest in their book and be willing to speak and travel.

For some reason, people think once they get their book on Amazon and in bookstores, they don't have to do anything else. This is so far from the truth. Everyone has to take an active role in promoting his or her book, and if they don't, they cannot expect to have a successful book project.

Another way of looking at this is the way a friend of mine outlined it in his book, **"Unlimited Possibilities"** about the difference between a leader and a manager. He says, you have to decide whether you are going to be the leader (visionary) or the manager. Here are the differences he lists in his book:

- **Leaders** are those who are given a vision/assignment to fulfill.
- **Managers** are those who are given a task to complete.

- **Leaders** have a long-term strategy.
- **Managers** live in the moment.

- **Leaders** see the big picture.
- **Managers** see the details.

- **Leaders** think outside the box.
- **Managers** maintain the status quo.

- **Leaders** rely on intuition.
- **Managers** rely on facts.

- **Leaders** see themselves as change agents
- **Managers** see themselves as stability agents.

He said, leadership is for everyone, and if you are going to be a leader, you can't be afraid to take a risk. It is the same in becoming an entrepreneur, you can't be afraid of failing. Sometimes you got to just do it. *No one should be pushing your vision more than you.*

Here is a declaration blessing that I confess over my life:

- I am wanted!

- I am wanted for my wisdom and counsel because I am smart, wise and intelligent!

- I am wanted by national radio and TV stations to share or talk about the goodness of God!

- I am wanted by corporate America, and big corporations will sign contracts with me for my consulting services and pay my professional fees!

- I am in heavy demand, which is opening up doors for TV and radio stations to offer me free air time and to host a regular program!

Bottom Line: You are not subject to this world!

Wealth Nugget From

This Chapter

Diligence

is the mother of good

fortune.

Recommended Books to Read

Born to Win By Zig Ziglar

Birthing Your Destiny by Dr. Shirley K. Clark

Show Me Your Three Closest Friends And I Will Show You Your Destiny

--The Late Bishop Mack Timberlake--

What many people have discovered who were poor growing up, and they are millionaires now is that everyone who comes with you or grows up with you **cannot** go with you. This can be a tough "pill to swallow" when often the people you have to release are dear friends and family members as your career expands.

The Late Bishop Mack Timberlake was an incredible leader and pastor. For almost ten years, I was under his leadership. He would often say, "Show me your three closest friends and I will show you your destiny." Now, that I have lived a half of century, I fully understand this saying. As I moved up the socio-economic ladder, I realized there was a vast difference in the mindsets of people from difference socio-economic backgrounds. So over the years, I have watched my associations change.

It is not that the people that were in my life were evil, but it is about different experiences and the law of attraction. People who have achieved a certain level of wealth see things differently than those who have not achieved the same. Millionaires think big, but most importantly, their associations often breed increase and wealth as well. I read once, every person you become connected to have other associations in their life just like them. It is true, everything you touch is touching something connected to it. This is why we are known as much for the people we avoid as the ones we associate with. Proverbs 13:20 says, "He who walks with the wise becomes wise, those who hang with fools become a fool."

When you hang out with people of influence and wealth, increase will inevitably follow. Life for those who are striving to become millionaires requires that we guard and manage the people we hang out with because you will never be bigger than the people you associate with on *a regular basis.* If millionaires are to be attracted to you or come into your life, then you need to understand wealth begets wealth. This has always amazed me. If you don't believe me, research rich people and you will find out most of their friends are people of wealth, power and influence like them. Wealth attracts wealth.

I can also speak very candidly about this area because this has been manifesting in my life for the past ten years, and even more so, the past four and half years (2009-2014). But what I did differently in the past four and a half years is that I only read books, listened to

CD's and watch DVD's by millionaires. And automatically, millionaires and people of influence came into my equation and began to embrace me, and people begin to give me things ordinarily I would have purchased.

Also, my income increased. Along with this, favor and created ideas flourished as I sat and talked with them. Right now, off the top of my head if I was to total up what all of these millionaires have sowed into my life monetarily; it is around $25,000. But the total of their influence on my life has been about $100,000; whether in cash, jewelry, larger business contracts, larger professional speaking fees, and expensive designer clothes, as well as tremendous favor with other millionaires and billionaires, etc. in a span of eight years.

So, yes, who you associate with can hinder or help your destiny. You are truly defined by the company you keep. This is a good time to evaluate the people around you and make some quality decisions to take the steps necessary to eliminate those who are not your **tribe.** Having money and success is not for the faint of heart. It takes just the same amount of tenacity to stay successful as it was becoming successful.

Also, one of the other reasons you have to watch who you hang out with is because hanging around the wrong people can hinder your blessing. Sometimes these people can even talk you out of it. By the time they finish telling you why something won't work, you can feel discouraged about going forward. I have definitely had this happen to me.

One time I had a great opportunity to increase my personal finances, but because there were some people around me with suspicious natures, my increased was delayed for months. Then God reminded me of the voices who were speaking into my spirit. They were people who had not achieved the level of success that I was after, nor were they wealthy or millionaires. They meant well, but I was listening to the wrong people.

The Late Bishop Mack Timberlake, Jr. was right, "Show me your three closest friends and I will show you your destiny." Choice your friends wisely because they are truly a mirror to the world of your destiny!

You want to associate with people who reflect the measure of prosperity you want to enjoy.

Wealth Nugget From

This Chapter

People who have achieved a certain level of wealth see things differently than those who have not achieved the same.

Recommended Books to Read

How to Win Friends and Influence People
by Dale Carnegie

Winning With People by John Maxwell

One isn't necessarily born with courage, but one is born with potential. Without courage, we cannot practice any other virtue with consistency.

--Maya Angelo--

I often say in my self-publishing book writing seminars that it takes courage to write a book. Because the moment you release a book, it has the potential of millions of eyes reading it, and not everyone will agree with your writing style or your grammatical choices.

We had a situation that happened like this years ago to one of our clients. A woman called my office to let me know that she found "**a**" grammatical error in one of our clients' book and she wanted to bring it to our attention. I told her she needed to contact the author because in this particular project we only assisted in the actual printing of the book. I lived in Texas and she was calling from Chicago just to tell us about "an" error. This is why I tell my authors that writing a book requires that you have thick skin. While many will not write a book, but there will be quite a few people on the sideline to show your flaws and how you could have done it better.

This is why success is not for the faint of heart, but for the courageous ones. When you choose to do what others will not do, you will always have what others will not have. I like what Financial Advisor, Dave Ramsey says, "If we would live like no one else, then we will live like no one else." And it does not matter whether you fail or succeed because the lesson(s) you have learned will continue to expand your horizon.

The secret to this model is consistency. You keep getting back up and trying again, and eventually an opportunity will avail itself. I read this saying somewhere that you are either going to be consistent or nonexistent. I choose to be consistent.

Truly, "One isn't necessarily born with courage, but one is born with potential. Without courage, we cannot practice any other virtue with consistency."

Listen, 80% of present day millionaires did not receive their fortune from an inheritance according to an article I read. Many of them were first time millionaires in their family lineage. In the book, **"One Minute Millionaire,"** it says that every 60 seconds someone in the world becomes a millionaire, and it only takes 1% of courage to become an entrepreneur and/or millionaire.

Who wants to become a millionaire? If this is you, it will take courage. You can't settle for what is comfortable or what feels good. You have to work outside of your comfort zone to be successful. One writer says it this way, **"Comfort is wicked!"** If you are the type of person that needs to know how every jot and tittle is going to work out before you take the plug into entrepreneurship, then you will probably never be an entrepreneur. You see, the word "entrepreneur" actually means risk taker. It means taking a risk for a sake of a profit. In order to have what you have never had, you have to do what you have never done.

For some people launching out into the deep and becoming an entrepreneur is easier than for others, but this does not mean the ones who do not have this "natural" proclivity cannot succeed as an entrepreneur. I like what Anthony Morrison says in his book, **"The Hidden Millionaire":**

> *It's true that some people are born with an ability to "think" like an entrepreneur, and these people have a definite advantage, but this way*

of thinking can be learned. It is simply a matter of following established principles and applying them to every endeavor. Anyone can be taught to think like or train themselves to think like an entrepreneur, and whether you're born with it or acquire the skill, once you have the right mindset and master these basic principles, success is just steps away. Whether you are driven by an entrepreneurial spirit or by a desire to improve your existing life and work situations, these principles are applicable to life in general."

Trusting your instincts is another way that will guide and enable you to take a bold step forward toward attaining your dream in life. The prize is always given to the ones who are in the race and not the ones on the sideline. Remember, hesitation only magnifies or enlarges fear.

Don't let familiarity hinder your financial opportunities! Be **BOLD** and **COURAGEOUS** like Maya Angelou states in her quote!!!

When you choose to do what others will not do, you will always have what others will not have.

Recommended Books to Read

Best Quotes by Maya Angelou

Wealth Is It Worth It? by S. Truett Cathy

Success Has A System, Manifestation Has A Method, and Production Has A Process

--Yvette Munroe--

am extremely excited about this quote because it comes from one of my dear friends, Yvette Munroe. It was in 2006 that Yvette's life radically changed when her business grossed over a million dollars. Yvette started out making $19,000 a year and now her net worth is over $10 million dollars. How did she do it? By being focused and intentional. This is what she means when she says success has a system, manifestation has a method and production has a process.

Yvette is a hard worker with an extraordinary understanding of the need to engage in activities that will produce a desired result. In her book, **"Holy Millionaire,"** she says, "A system is a set of connected parts forming a desired outcome." She also goes on to say:

> *The system of success is a set of parts when engaged together will always work to produce the same result. The system of success is intentional whether or not the participant is conscious of it or not. Using the system, you can predict the results. A key component of success is a clearly articulated vision. The common use of articulate is spoken words...I have met countless people who tell me they have a vision, but when we get right down to it many of them have not yet clarified their vision. Usually people say, "I want to own...or do such and such." They are steeped in the activity, but they rarely*

can tell you why and when they do it. Often what they do, does not line up with their lives as articulated through their behaviors controlled by misguided principles.

A clear vision makes it easy to see what the end will be. It will be easy to be understood by others, readily able to be taken advantage of and held without effort. A clear vision tells everyone what is important. It is value driven. A clear vision is location focused. It tells everyone where you are and where you want to be. It is result-oriented. It says what will be produced and who will benefit. A good vision statement identifies the primary goal/purpose of this activity, therefore, making it easy for steps or strategies to be employed along a path that leads in a fixed direction.

Therefore being intentional provides energy within your dream that illuminates and inspires created ideas to get the job done or get the desired results. These created ideas are the manifestations of the method, which are progenitors of the intentional system leading us toward the production of process.

The production of process is faith and patience. The thing that we long to have must exist in the invisible realm first long before we see the manifestation in the natural. **You must see it, before you see it.** Yvette says, "Our purpose is inside of us and as we produce our purpose, it will propel us to the wealthy place where the transfer of wealth will happen."

Just before I started writing this book, I read an article by Tom Corley on the internet about 20 things the rich do every day. Most rich people are intentional people. Here is a list of intentional things that most rich people do every day:

1. Rich people eat less junk food everyday.

2. Rich people focus on a single goal.

3. Rich people exercise at least 4 days a week.

4. Rich people listen to audio books as they commute to work.

5. Rich people maintain to-do list.

6. Rich people make their children read 2 or more nonfiction books a month.

7. Rich people make their children do volunteer work at least 10 hours or more a month.

8. Rich people make happy birthday calls.

9. Rich people write down their goals.

10. Rich people read 30 minutes or more each day for education or career reasons.

11. Rich people speak what is on their minds.

12. Rich people network five hours or more each month.

13. Rich people watch one hour or less of TV every day.

14. Rich people watch very little reality shows.

15. Rich people wake up three hours before their work day.

16. Rich people teach good daily success habit to their children.

17. Rich people believe good habits create opportunities.

18. Rich people believe bad habits create detrimental bad luck.

19. Rich people believe in lifelong learning.

20. Rich people love to read.

So as we can see rich people are truly focused and intentional individuals who do not leave their success up to chance. They take and make tangible steps daily to maintain and sustain their wealth aptitude. We must do the same if we want the same results. A few years ago, I was in a meeting where a millionaire was sharing and one of the things he said that stuck with me is that principles work every time. If it is not a principle, you will not get the desired result, but if it is a principle, you will get the desired result every time. Purpose connected with principles will produce a product.

Wealth Nugget From This Chapter

Being intentional provides energy within your dream that illuminates and inspires created ideas to get the job done or get the desired results.

Recommended Book to Read

Holy Millionaire by Yvette Munroe

The Hidden Millionaire by Anthony Morrison

You Cannot

Expect Victory And

Plan For Defeat

--Joel Osteen--

When I think about this quote, I think about all the "good" things many people do to prepare for a "rainy" day or death, such as preparing a will or buying life insurance. I think we will probably all agree these are good ideas, but the main objective behind each of these is to be cared for when bad things happen. I am in total agreement with this, but sometimes people are more focused on taking care of their future than living in the present moment.

There is no substitute to living in the NOW! It is your **now** moment that will give life to your tomorrow, and inevitably your future, so you might as well enjoy life today.

Everything cannot be about planning for the bad days or rainy days. Therefore, you need to have a plan for good day as well. Every day you should wake up vibrant and excited about the impact you are going to have on the world that day and not vice versa.

Victory is a positive energy, and because it is a positive force, when it is generated the mind and body secrete a "happy" chemical -- an "expect to win" attitude. It invites the world to dance with you, and even though the world might have a different rhythm, it is the giddy component of your victory anthem that properly aligns this unwelcome trajectory with the lyrics of your day.

I believe this is what Joel Osteen is trying to get us to operate out of. He wants us to function out of or make decisions from a mindset of triumph and victory, instead of fear and defeat. We need to stop looking for the "hammer" to come down in our lives, but rather we need to be looking for favor to surround our lives.

Too many of us worry about things that we can't change. Worry debilitates emotions. It disrupt your peace and when your peace is disrupted, this will affect your performance.

Many people spend 92% of their emotional energies over things that won't happen or things they can't change.

There was a study done by Dr. Walter Cavet about worry. He found out that 40% of the things we worry about never happen; 30% of our worry is about things that happened in the past; 12% of our worries are needless about our health; 10% of our worries were insignificant or petty (things that will not make much difference in our lives one way or another). So many people spend

92% of their emotional energies over things that won't happen or things they can't change. This is ridiculous! Only 8% of things that happen to us in life are legitimate challenges.

So if you are one of those people who worry a lot, here are some things you can do to alleviate stress and worry in your life, according to author, Brenda Denson in her book, **"Stress-Proof Your Life: 121 Fun & Creative Stress Zippers"**:

> ➤ **Start a family tree:** We all have something about our history that we want to know more about. Spend quality time interviewing family members to learn more about your family tree.

> ➤ **Learn to play an instrument:** If you don't have time to join a conservatory for lessons, there are inexpensive software programs that will introduce you to learning to play an instrument.

➢ **Get a Massage:** Treat yourself to some "Me-Time." Enjoy a 30 to 60 minute massage.

➢ **Try a new hair style:** Try a new hair color or style. This might give you a new outlook on life.

➢ **Test drive an expensive luxury car:** Visit a luxury car dealership and test drive their top of the line vehicle. This will help expand your world and your mental capacity for greatness.

➢ **Vacation get-aways:** Search online for last minute travel deals and find a great deal for a 3-4 day vacation.

➢ **Go see a play:** Go to a local theatre and see a live play.

➢ **Tour your city:** You will be amazed at how many people live in their city for years and have never toured the sites.

➢ **Blow Bubbles:** Go to a local park and sit on the bench and blow bubbles. She said you might want to take a child with you, so you won't look strange to others.

This is just a few ways you can relax, and hopefully, limit how much mental energy you spend on worrying. But regardless, we must manage our external surroundings to make sure they do not override our present success moments. We have to do things that reinforce our successful state of being, and this is especially true when our external surroundings are filled with negative energy.

I know when we are faced with a harsh reality, we sometimes want to switch our thinking or behavior based on these circumstances. But if we participate in activities contrary to our belief, values and hopes, we will produce outcomes that are undesirable. Remember, opportunities lie in the decisions we make. But also, defeat lies in the decisions we make.

As well, we need to monitor who we allow to speak into our lives. If we lend our ears to listen to unwise voices or people with limited, erroneous information, then we will make decisions from a misguided standpoint versus a platform of victory. I want to close this section with a story I read about four blind men that depicts this point explicitly.

If we lend our ears to listen to unwise voices or people with limited, erroneous information, then we will make decisions from a misguided standpoint versus a platform of victory.

The story goes that four blind men encountered an elephant and in their attempts to describe what they had encountered, they each touched different parts of the elephant's body.

One said, "It was a palm leaf," because he was touching the elephant's flat ears.

Another said, "No, it is a tree trunk," because he was touching the elephant's leg.

The next one said, "No, you both are wrong, it is a snake," because he was holding the tail of the elephant.

Finally, the last one said, "All of you are stupid; it is a stone wall because it is strong and sturdy," because he was leaning on the elephant's massive body.

The moral of this story is when someone advises you, always know what part of the elephant he or she is touching. Don't build plans around a description that is, in fact, a narrow perspective based on someone's limited knowledge of the whole. You want to make sure the person has a global understanding of the situation.

If you plan for success, then think like a victorious person – an overcomer. There is nothing wrong with having a contingency program (any smart leader should have one), but your focus should be more on succeeding than failing.

Wealth Nugget From This Chapter

*There is no substitute to living in the NOW! It is your **now** moment that will give life to your tomorrow, and inevitably your future.*

Recommended Books to Read

Break Out by Joel Osteen

Act Like A Success, Think Like A Success
by Steve Harvey

Expect to Win by Carla Harris

Wealth Is Not For Self

--Dr. Larry Holley--

Sharing will always create more. I know this may sound like an oxymoron, but it is something about the law of reciprocity, which is a success model. If you study the life of wealthy people, they are always giving to some charitable cause. While I believe, we all should desire to live financially independent, we must also keep our mind focused on the fact that true success lies in our legacies. It lies in our giving.

When you have died and gone on, people will remember your humanitarian contributions and attributes more than your marketplace gifting. Maya Angelou says it best, "I've learned that people will forget what you said, people will forget what you did, but people will never forget how you made them feel."

You see, "wealth is more than money. It is fullness to the overflow until you can feed others off of you," according to millionaire, Yvette Munroe. When God blesses you with abundance, life is too short for you not to pay it forward.

This is what I love about Dr. Larry A. Holley and how he thinks about money. Since receiving his millions, he is now spending his life helping others acquire wealth or large sums of money by coaching and partnering with others to bless their church, ministry, organization and/or business.

Dr. Holley's specialty area is buying real estate – large and small office buildings and shopping strips. In fact, he is a real estate mogul.

His ministry is call, **"Millionaires With A Mission."** He also has a church funding group, of which the Wealth Coach of his team, Patricia Enright-Gray, shows people how to stop having "lazy" money. This means, money that is not working for you. She truly believes that your money should be working as hard for you as you are working for it. Patricia is an expert in helping people make their money work for them instead of them working for it. Patricia is so sharp and tenacious in finding your money.

Dr. Holley also has an excellence acquisition business consultant, Bernard Drew, on his team. He is phenomenal in negotiating with bankers and other financial institutions. He takes care of all the details in securing properties for Dr. Holley and he makes sure all the sales are finalized. Dr. Holley has a wonderful executive team that he has put together.

Also, Dr. Holley is one of the most humble men I know, and he is truly "the millionaire next door." While he is a multi-millionaire, he doesn't spend his money on overpriced garments, shoes, jewelry, etc., anymore. He uses his money for missions and other humanitarian acts of kindness.

I have seen him give away thousands of dollars randomly to people in the audience during his training while raising money for someone else's "cause." He does this all the time. His famous saying is, "Wealth is not for self." Meaning, we are blessed to be a blessing.

This does not mean we are supposed to live in shacks or rundown buildings. In fact, he has a beautiful home. Winston Churchill says it this way, "We make a living by what we get, but we make a life by what we give."

At the time of meeting Dr. Holley, it had been my desire to meet someone that could "take me by the hand" and show me how to buy office buildings and shopping centers. This is exactly what he did. Dr. Holley owns over 50 office buildings and shopping strips. I am so grateful to have met him.

Giving is a part of living and loving. It is a force that ignites joy into the hearts of the recipients and the givers as well. It has the power to lift you up. Sowing positions you for promotion. The Bible says it this way, "Your gift will make room for you and bring you before great people." Many people want to be in the company of great people. Well, one of the ways, according to the Bible, to attaining this goal is giving.

Dr. Holley has the right formula for good success. I think we all know that every success is not good success. Giving to someone less fortunate than you or helping someone in a crisis, is a formula for good success. Listen, poor people complain about giving, but most rich people give freely. Which one are you?

Give freely and become

more wealthy; be stingy and lose

everything.

Proverbs 11:24 (NLT)

Sowing positions

you for promotion.

Recommended Books to Read

Pray & Grow Richer by Dr. Shirley K. Clark

Building Generational Wealth
by Anna & Richmond McCoy

Rich People Educate Themselves, Poor People Entertain Themselves.

--Myron Golden--

This book is a result of this wealth wisdom principle. As I was sitting at my computer going through emails one morning, I noticed I got an email from someone named Dennis Cummins inviting me to register for his upcoming webinar in a couple of days. I looked at the topic. It sounded interesting, so I registered for it. It was a webinar about self-publishing books, and since this was my industry, I was curious.

However, I knew it was going to be challenging for me to remember to get on the call because it was set for 8pm on a Wednesday night. I usually shut my work day down by 6pm if not earlier, so I knew I would have to work at remembering to get on the call.

For me most days I am up between 3am to 5am, so it was going to be a challenge. But for some reason, I felt I really needed to stay focused and make a conscious effort to make this webinar. And believe me, it was challenging. I was so tired by 8:00pm, and this was the time it started, that I knew that I was not going to be able to watch it on my PC or laptop. So I thought, I wonder if there was a call-in number, and there was. I secured the number, crawled into my bed, dialed into the conference call line, and laid the phone on the bed next to me, while I listened to Dennis.

As I listened to Dennis Cummins, he said something in the first 30 minutes that I had never thought about. He said, "You don't have to be a millionaire to write about being a millionaire." I said to myself, "Hmm." He gave further examples of how you can do this whether you are a millionaire or not. All the "bells and whistles" went off inside of me.

You see, what Dennis did not know was that I wanted to write a book that the word, "millionaire" would be in the title. But the mere fact that I was not a millionaire, I assumed gave me no right to write something like this. However, when he said, "You don't have to be a millionaire to write about being a millionaire," and gave examples, my "baby" leaped inside of me so much so that this book was birthed 24 hours later.

This is what being a lifelong student is all about. You never know where your "next" idea is going to come from, your next opportunity, your next breakthrough, and/or your next increase. But just by me putting myself in a position to continue to learn and be trained by Dennis Cummins on his webinar, another book was birthed inside of me. Thanks Dennis for your impact on my life.

Educating yourself constantly is a must if you are going to be rich and **stay** rich. There is never a time you can stop learning. In fact, when you wake up each day, you should make sure you go to school. I know this is what I do. It is said that wealthy people read books on things they won't need for years. But poor people or people with a poverty mentality only read books when they need the information.

Every day I awake I try to learn something new. I want my brain cells to be constantly stimulated – be constantly in a state of growing. "When you want to reach solid conclusions and not tentative theories, then you must be willing to risk what you know for what you want to know," says millionaire and New York Times Best-Selling Author, Bishop T. D. Jakes. It is definitely true that instinct operates most accurately when you have as much data as possible. This is why you can function more "wholely" in your thinking when you have given art and science the "green" light to create a navigational system in your brain to function at its optimum level. You see, every missed opportunity can cost you millions of dollars. So this is why we need to prepare constantly. ***Preparation brings about manifestation.***

In my book, ***"Pray & Grow Richer,"*** I give some startling statistics of how most people lack discipline in reading books. You might want to purchase this book because I know you are going to be shocked like I was when I saw the statistics. Bottom line: Most people don't read.

If you are broke and living from paycheck to paycheck, and you have a choice to go to the movies or attend a financial workshop and you select going to the movies, then you are, perhaps, like the saying – *Poor people entertain themselves.* Successful people prepare for life, poor people react to life. You can never over prepare!

Myron Golden also says, "If you are not making $25,000 a month, then you need to throw your TV away." But if you want to see who you really are just check your checkbook ledger or your debt/credit card statement. What do you mostly spend your money on? If you spent most of your money on things in the entertainment industry, then you are operating in a principle that will keep you in lack and poverty. However, if most of your money was spent on things that help you create wealth, then eventually wealth will find its way to your house. On the next page is a poem that I discovered on the internet about "knowing," which says it all.

I Know Everything

There is something I don't know

That I am supposed to know.

I don't know what it is I don't know,

And yet I am supposed to know,

And I feel I look stupid

If I seem both not to know it

And not know what it is I don't know.

Therefore, I pretend I know it.

This is nerve-wracking since...

I don't know what I must pretend to know.

Therefore, I pretend I know everything.

By Ronald Laing, "Knots" (1970)

Stupid people pretend to know everything?

I hope this is not you – stupid! But just in case you are not sure, you might want to take the student evaluation test on the next page, and let it be the final voice to speak into your life. Please select the best answer that describes your lifestyle.

Now, you have to be honest with yourself because it will not work if you don't. Remember, this is just an assessment tool to help you come face to face with the real you. It is not what you say in public that is important. It is what you say to yourself in private.

STATEMENT	Put a check by the answer that best describes you
A. When I am on the internet I spend most of my time gaming, on Facebook or watching movies on YouTube.	
B. When I am on the internet I spend most of my time researching information and learning how to acquire a new skill.	
A. When I have an option to attend a seminar on finance versus going to a recreation activity, I go out and have fun.	
B. When I have an option to attend a seminar on finance versus going to a recreation activity, I go to the seminar.	
A. I might start out reading a book or periodical, but I never finish it.	
B. I read at least one book or periodical a month to its completion.	
A. I sleep late because people don't know how hard I work.	
B. I rise early almost every morning to meditate, read and prepare for my day.	

If your answers fell mostly in the "a" category, then you need to begin as soon as possible to work on doing the things in the "b" category if you desire to be rich. The "a" category are habits of poor people. The "b" category are habits of rich people.

Also, before I close this section, I want to address another point. Having a formal education is not being a lifelong learner or student. Sometimes people put too much stock in formal education than continuing education. If you can acquire financial freedom with just formal education, then most people in our society would be financially independent or wealthy. But on the contrary, this is not so. Most people who retire around age 65, retire broke, so the system, as is, is not a system designed to make you rich. And if this is true, and it is, then just getting a formal education is not the answer.

Here is a startling piece of information you might not know. Forty-two percent of all college graduates never read another book after college. This is a shame! You would think a college graduate would know the importance of reading and the effect it would have on their mind **when failing to do so.**

Hmm...interesting, I thought these were educated people! So being educated does not guarantee that you will make great life decisions. This is what I am talking about.

When I was attending a Six-Figure Business Seminar, I bought a CD from one of the speakers, who was a millionaire. As I was listening to the CD, the speaker said one month he spent over $3000 on products to learn from, but he extracted one idea that made his business $80,000.

Yes, I know, having a formal education is good, and I believe in it wholeheartedly, but in order to reach success beyond the basic America dream, we have to be lifelong learners. You owe it to yourself to be all you can imagine.

*Educating yourself constantly is a must if you are going to be rich and **stay** rich.*

Recommended Books to Read

From Trash Man to Cash Man by Myron Golden

Secrets of the Millionaire Mind
By T. Harv Eker

Dress The Way You Want To Be Addressed

--Dr. Nasir Siddiki--

Within the first few days of starting to write this book, I had the opportunity to operate in this wealth wisdom by Dr. Nassir Siddiki. Dr. Siddiki is another unique millionaire that is one of my mentors.

Dr. Siddiki travels weekly throughout the world teaching people about financial wealth. I think one of the extraordinary things that I heard about Dr. Siddiki is his testimony. He was sick to death and his entire face was covered with hideous boils and sores from shingles. Yet, after going through an ordeal like this, he never gave up on life, so much so that when he was healed, he became an even more shrewd business man. And in five years, he made $300 million dollars.

For months I had been reviewing my financial portfolio to see where I stood for retirement and for other possible business opportunities. And since it had been only a month since I looked at one of my stock investments, I decided to go online and open up a free online account to see the latest balance in this account.

Well, as I was trying to set everything up, it would not go through. As instructed by the auto response, it said call the representative. I did, but the representative could not resolve the problem. In fact, he could not find my account, therefore, he could not find my money. He recommended that I go to one of their local offices and see what they could do, and I did.

But when I was getting dressed, I heard my mentor, Dr. Nassir Siddiki's voice, "Dress the way you want to be addressed." I think the first time Dr. Siddiki shared this with me was about a year and a half prior to this and from time to time this statement would cross my mind. However, it was more of a passing thought. But this time, it stood out more profoundly. So I immediately upgraded my garment and left to go to my financial investment company.

I was treated with such professional care and significance when I was serviced. Even though initially, the customer service assistant had problems locating my account and money, she forged on until she found someone who could assist me. She assured me in the process, she would take care of it, and she did. This is what being dressed the way you want to be addressed can get you – conscientious assistance and great customer service. Sometimes we have to dress "in authority," so that we don't have to assert authority.

Now for some, this might be petty, but you would not go to a job interview with tattered and torn jeans. I hope you would not. You would dress appropriately. You would dress for success. One of my millionaire mentors was quite perturbed with one of his mentees because of how he dressed at a formal event. He shared with me that he told this individual that he didn't have the luxury of dressing down based on the state of his finances. He told him when you get your millions, then you can dress anyway you want, but right now you need to dress appropriately, so that he could attract people with money. While the millionaires can dress the way that they want, you cannot. He was quite perturbed with this young man.

I knew going into the financial institution that I wanted to be treated with respect and dignity, and my subconscious knew it, and reminded me of this saying.

I am so glad I listened because everything worked out without any harsh words being spoken or it becoming a challenging situation. Remember, sometimes we have to dress the way we want to be addressed. Also, sometimes when we look important, it helps us think important. It is true, your physical exterior affects your mental interior.

There are certain garments that I wear that somehow make me feel more important, or I have more confidence when I wear them versus some of the other garments hanging in my closet. So when I am going places that I am not sure about, I usually put on a garment that boosts my confidence and self-esteem. Therefore, I feel armed in the midst of uncertainties. And I always come out on top when I do this.

Your appearance has a voice, and it tells people what to think about you. So make sure it says what you want it to say. You should never leave home guessing whether or not you look like the kind of person you want to be. Conclusion: Dress Right! Most of the time you have only one opportunity to make a good impression. The better you are "packaged," the better you will be accepted by people in general.

Respect your appearance!!!

Your appearance has a voice, and it tells people what to think about you, so make sure it says what you want it to say.

Recommended Books to Read

Kingdom Principles of Financial Increase

by Dr. Nassir Siddiki

You Don't Need A Title To Be A Leader

by Mark Sanborn

When

People Show You

Themselves, Believe

Them.

--Oprah Winfrey--

Boy, I have been learning this lesson over the last few years – *"When people show you who they are, believe them."* It is always my desire to give people the benefit of the doubt. But by doing this, I had been overriding this statement, and I have been getting "bitten" repeatedly.

The first time I heard this saying, Oprah Winfrey was saying it on her show. But later I heard she got this from her dear friend, the late Maya Angelou. But since I heard it from Oprah first, I will give her the credit for the sake of this book.

Just before writing this book, I had to come to this conclusion with several close friends. I had some things happen to me that some friends were a part of which was quite unusual. It put me in a place where I had to re-examine the relationship I had with them. It was hard because I just did not want to believe this was their nature. But because I didn't re-examine my relationship with them, certain things happened again similar to the previous behavior. So I failed the lesson, and I had to learn the lesson again. Listen, when people show you who they are, trust me, believe them. As another friend told me, "Dr. Clark, a leopard can't change its spots."

"Many people will want to use your mouth to convey their message. Don't let them. Others will try to harness your influence for their agenda. Resist them.

There will be moments when someone steals your thunder, mauls your paws and nips your nose. But you can always survive the treacheries and tragedies if you have a base to which you can return…. Always know your base, that calm core of confidence within you, and how to access it and take shelter as needed," according to Bishop T. D. Jakes.

This is what was happening in my situation. I was using not just my mouth to further their message, but my time, resources and business. I didn't mind helping my friends get ahead, but when their motives were no longer pure, then I had to make a choice to move on. I had to release them. This was a hard pill to swallow, but I passed the test.

Why do we keep putting ourselves in situations where we are being taken advantage of? Today, if this is you, stop the madness. Make a decision and release these people. It could be a love one, friend, spouse or boss. There will be another friend. There will be another boss and their definitely can be another spouse. Now, I am not advocating you get a divorce, but you can exclude them out of any further endeavors in a diplomatic way. But you have to get these toxic people out of your life before you are elevated in your business. If not, they will become a big distraction as you are succeeding in life.

Everybody is not your "tribe." The problem I dealt with was the people I had to release resembled my tribe so very closely that I couldn't always discern their motives. Plus, I was doing things with them that I felt assured I was supposed to do. However, what I realized later was that God was using them to position me for greater works and opportunities. This did not mean I had to stay with them, but He took the situation and made it good for me. When I saw this, I said, "WOW!"

Let me say this. When you have to release people that you have an invested in there will be a ripping in your heart. For me, I always have internal tears regarding these types of releases, but I had to learn how to *master* and *manage* my heart.

Now, the ripping wasn't because of the disappointment of what they did, but because it stopped me from doing what I wanted to do for them. You see, I saw myself blessing them over and over again, and it truly hurts my heart when I cannot give my gift (me) fully to my "tribe". So it is going to hurt, but it will pass. The thing you have to do is stay focused and keep pursuing your dreams and vision. You have to know that God has another connection for you that you don't know right now. It is truly in the invisible realm. I have no idea who and what I am going to connect with next and all I am going to do in the future, but I know it is BIG.

How do I know this, because in order for me to do what I am called to do, big doors and big opportunities will have to open, which will lead to my *wealthy* place. And if you will stay focused, continue to think BIG, you will win in the end also.

Say this with me:

I AM UNSTOPPABLE!

I AM NOT CONFUSED ABOUT MY DESTINY!!!

Everybody is not your "tribe."

Recommended Books to Read

Words That Matter by The Oprah Magazine

The Magic of Thinking Big by David J. Schwartz, Ph.D.

You Must

Become The Architect

Of Your Own

Dream

--Anna McCoy--

ever leave your success up to chance. Only one in 14 million wins the lottery. It is time you create your own world. And I repeat, never let anyone create your world because they will always create it too small.

Coach Anna McCoy – everybody needs a Coach Anna McCoy in their life. She has an organization called,

"Woman Act Now," and this is what she spends her life doing – encouraging all to do and manifest in the now. If you are ever in her presence, she has an infectious personality that makes everyone feels comfortable and appreciated. In fact, if you call her and happened to get her voicemail, she closes out her voicemail saying, *"You are loved and appreciated."*

Anna and her husband, Richmond are founding partners of UrbanAmerica, a multibillion dollar private real estate equity fund that purchases and revitalizes inner-city commercial properties. Yet, regardless of their success they are approachable and they encourage everyone to dream without limits. They are such a power couple that I am amazed at their business acumen and their ability to generate wealth. I read once that effective leaders focus not only on building a brand, but on building relationships. This is definitely Coach Anna's philosophy in life. Don't get me wrong, she is a brilliant international business consultant, but her heart is always with the people.

The times I have stayed in her home and spoken with her on the phone are priceless. When I am around people like Anna I want to "pick" their brains and hear how they created wealth -- what makes them tick? But one thing I have learned about Coach Anna McCoy is that she wants us to dream big, and then go after our dreams.

In her book, **"Woman Act Now,"** this is how she says it: *"Start executing your dream today, no matter how large or small it may seem. You owe it to yourself. Take the risk of telling others what you will do and then do it! It's time to act! It's time to launch and live your dream."* She encourages all to do whatever is in our hearts to do, to do it **NOW!** So perhaps:

- It's time to go after that new job.
- It's time to start that business.
- It's time to expand your horizon.
- It's time to get that degree you always wanted.
- It's time to apply for a passport.

- It's time to write that book.

- It's time to take that cruise.

- It's time to record that CD.

- It's time to increase you product line.

- It's time to buy that new computer.

- It's time to start that magazine you have always wanted to start.

Do something every day towards your vision. A doer will always have a propensity for action rather than passivity. In Anna's book, she outlines ten keys for successful execution. I have listed the ten keys below, however, I am not going fully into the details about each. If you want to know more, buy the book.

Here are the ten keys:

1. **Choices are everything in life** – Your choices and decisions connect the dots of execution, so you need to master making right choices.

2. **Value differences** – You have to value differences to avoid doing things the same way all the time.

3. **Overcome internal struggles** – Positive self-talk will help you to excel in execution.

4. **Vision is seeing plainly and clearly where you are going** – Effective execution plans are well-written.

5. **Verify and follow up** – Verify and follow up are two essence principles when delegating tasks to others.

6. **Patience and diligence, like faith, move mountains** – Patience and diligence will carry you through the gap of execution.

7. **Performance is a requirement** – Being a passive person is detrimental to execution.

8. **Don't assume...Ask** – Clarify everything.

9. **Always be honest** – Honesty is the best policy, avoid trying to cover up mistakes.

10. **Keep your word** – Be a person of your word. If you say you are going to do something, do it.

Don't ever let anyone stop you from dreaming. Use your imagination and execution power to create your future. A dreamer will always be the architect of ideas, moving them from one dimension to the next until they are manifested in the physical dimension. And in case you don't know it, your dream has the ability and power within to generate wealth, cure diseases and advance careers. Dreamers see beyond what exists in the natural. Their limitations are never the sky.

As I was researching this topic on the internet, I ran into an article that talked about something that the writer called a wealth map. It stated that the way money affects people is based on three standpoints: **Auditory, Visual and Incidental Programming**. The way we think about money depends on these three forms of programming.

Auditory -- What did you hear growing up about money? **Visual** -- How did you see your family handle money? **Incidental** -- Was there a tragic incident that might have damaged your mindset about money and success? Whatever occurred, the writer said, these three programs coded it into your brain, affecting the way you respond to money now. If you were programmed that money is evil or you can never get ahead; then you will never succeed in life until you address and correct this mindset. You can be successful, you just have to get rid of this erroneous mindset and believe that you are going to be successful. Always remember, we cannot allow our perception of circumstances to form our reality.

"The middle of the road is where the white
line is – and that's the worst place to drive."
--Robert Frost

"A man is not old until regrets take
the place of dreams."
--John Barrymore

Many people listen to prosperity CD's, watch videos on money and financial management and attend financial seminars, but it does not affect their financial situation. The problem is in their mind as well as their belief system. We have to shift our thinking and our core belief if we want to attract money and be successful.

Successful people think success, not failure!

Wealth Nugget From

This Chapter

Do something every day towards your vision. A doer will always have a propensity for action rather than passivity.

Recommended Books to Read

Woman Act Now by Coach Anna McCoy

Financial Prosperity by Dr. Pat Francis

I've Never Had A Hater Who's Doing Better Than Me

--Bishop T. D. Jakes

I am so excited to have the opportunity to share with you about this millionaire, Bishop T. D. Jakes, and how his sayings and teachings have affected my life. Besides being my pastor for over 18 years (1996-2015), he has also been my coach, teacher, and business consultant from afar. I am truly a grateful spiritual daughter and extremely honored to have had the privilege of being under his tutelage for so many years. When I think of Bishop Jakes, I think of this scripture, *"The one who guards a fig tree will eat its fruit, and whoever protects their master will be honored"* (Proverbs 27:18 NIV). I don't let anyone talk about Bishop Jakes. When you know someone's story and the journey to his or her success, it gives you a better perspective of where a person is now. Do I understand everything Bishop Jakes does, no, I don't, but it does not negate the fact that I would forever be grateful for his impartation and impact on my life.

When Bishop Jakes moved to the Dallas, TX area, where I live, he came with an extraordinary message and mindset. And what was one of the unique components about him right away was that he came having his "own" money. You see, in the clergy community most pastors are usually one or two paychecks away from being broke and homeless. I know some people take great glory in seeing preachers broke and begging, but I have learned this is not the will of God for His servants. And I am not sure completely why these dichotomies exist, when we see many rich people in the Bible serving God and all their needs were met. But the most incredible thing we often overlook about these rich people is that they all are entrepreneurs and business owners.

Working a job will never get you rich unless you have stock options and the company you work for is one like Microsoft, Google or Facebook. The sooner you recognize this, the sooner you can begin to reprogram your mind to change. The Bible says a man that does not work is like an infidel. What it does not say is that you should be working for someone else. As long as we are working for someone else, we are making them rich and not ourselves.

Now back to Bishop Jakes. When Bishop Jakes moved to the Dallas area from Charleston, WV, he impacted the region like a whirlwind. His stellar preaching and business acumen caught the attention of so many people of wealth, influence and power. While he was so excited about these opportunities, there were others who were not.

Bishop Jakes was not unfamiliar with "haters" or people who didn't like him because of this or that, but as he moved up the ladder, this type of hatred intensified. And as a member and a leader in his church, when this first started happening, there were times I could see him being slightly frustrated. However, his tenacity to stay focused and to forge on, regardless of opposition, was outstanding. From the time he first moved to Dallas until now, his resume has become a "class act." I have seen God do mighty things for him. Here are some of his accomplishments:

- ➢ He has been a **New York Times Best-Selling author** over and over again.
- ➢ **He is an executive producer of movies** seen at theaters.
- ➢ He had his **own talk show on BET network.**

- He **produced a traveling play** called, "Woman Thou Art Loosed."
- He has been on the **cover of Times and Essence Magazine** and many others.
- He has been featured on the **Oprah Winfrey Show,** and has led a training for her global classroom experience.
- And he hosted one of the **nation's largest conference meetings, which attracted almost 100,000 people** when it first launched in Atlanta, GA – MegaFest.

For the members of his church, we have taken this journey with him, and we are so **Godly** proud of our "Papa." We celebrate him and his accomplishments. The reason so many of us can celebrate him is that we have seen him endure so much because of the level of success he is experiencing. But he never let "haters" divert his focus from his first love -- the people God has given him to pastor. His heart is truly with his congregants, and now he can care less what his "haters" are saying.

In his book, **"Instinct,"** he says:

"People ahead of you, living in the liberty of instinct—guided uniqueness, will welcome you, encourage you, and mentor you. They will inspire you to be a pioneer and not a poser. Only those incarcerated by their unwillingness to listen to their instincts and to take the risks required for success will seek to deter you."

He also says, "Whenever you're thrust into the wild, someone or something will immediately pick up your scent and make strategic decisions regarding their response to your arrival. The agendas are endless, the enemies everywhere, and allies often apathetic. Fan clubs and fight clubs are met on the same street corner. The difference between a friend and a foe can be as subtle as the distinction between identical twins. That is to say, you can scarcely tell them apart!...It is a science...It's a laboratory experiment to discover what you can and cannot say. It's listening to your instincts as well as the insinuations of your new associates. And learning in the lab remains dangerous, since not all chemicals mix well! Chemical reactions can produce powerful results that either destroy or create energy for the organization."

Bishop Jakes tells us in this book that every jungle has predators. And if you are going to survive, it will require that you know your own proclivities and preferences, your default settings and disciplines. You also have to know the difference between accelerate and acclimate. There are times in your success elevation that your main objective should be acclimation instead of acceleration. Always remember as you move up the ladder and you find yourself in a new environment, the individuals that have already been occupying that space know things that you don't know. Let your ears and eyes be your learning tools and instruments. Sometimes we talk too much. While we are excited about our new environment, don't ever forget it might be a "trial" run for you. But regardless, predators can exist in every realm of your exaltation.

But the thing you must do to keep on track is to keep your focus. Let your internal drive or passion be your focus when the external is in turmoil. Remember what Bishop Jakes said, "He had never had a hater that was doing better than him." Haters truly are the best evidence that you are succeeding.

You see, he who wins the race cannot run with the pack. There will always be dream killers -- people who are mad that you succeeded; people who are mad that you had an idea that they did not have; and people who are mad that you did this or that. The bottom line:

Unfulfilled people mess with other people. Since they cannot realize their own dreams, they have to kill yours.

And don't forget to watch those who claim they have your back. If not, you could end up on your back. We have to hear more instinctively who our true tribe members are. These are the individuals you want to build with. These are the dream fulfillers that have been ordained to assist you in realizing your next level of success. Truly, no man is an island. I like the way Mark Victor Hansen outline this in his book, **"One Minute Millionaire."** He says, you need **"A Dream, A Team and A Theme"**.

The Dream – What is that you want to do?
> ➢ <u>For Mark:</u>   Building millionaire mind-sets in people.

The Team – Finding individuals that can assist with the dream.

> ➤ <u>For Mark:</u> Attracting mentors, masterminding partners to help make your dream a reality.

The Theme – What is the overall operational success strategy to make it happen?

> ➤ <u>For Mark:</u> Selecting and applying one or more basic millionaire models for making money fast.

He also believes in the **Be, Do** and **Have** principles.

- **BE** an enlightened millionaire
- **DO** what is needed to be done
- **HAVE** the desired outcome

Your success is not predicated on your haters or disgruntled fans, it is up to you. Don't forget what Mark Victor Hansen said, the day **YOU** decide to become wealthy, the universe will cheerfully provide. Mark made over $143 million dollars on a book series no one initially wanted to publish, the "Chicken Soup for the Soul" collection.

Responding to Critics

Now, I know sometimes we have to respond to our critics. Recently, I just read an article on how to respond to critics by Mike Bonem. Mike is a consultant, author, speaker, church leader, businessman, husband and father. Mike has spent over 10 years on the staff of West University Baptist Church in Houston, most recently as Executive Pastor. His business endeavors have included consulting as a senior manager with McKinsey & Company, one of the world's leading management consulting firms, and senior leadership roles in two environmental service companies. Mike obtained his M.B.A. degree, with distinction, from Harvard Business School, after having obtained a B.S. degree in chemical engineering from Rice University.

He said what a leader should keep in mind when responding to criticism is five things:

1. ***No one is above criticism.*** Regardless who we are, someone is going to misunderstand us and our motives.

2. ***Criticism doesn't mean that you've done the wrong thing.*** You can do the right thing, but doing the right thing does not always equate to the lack of criticism or complaints. But one thing I do like what Mike said is that we should consider whether our critics have a legitimate point, but don't back down just to appease them. I heard executive movie producer, Tyler Perry and billionaire mogul, Oprah Winfrey say the same thing.

3. ***Critics may only know part of the truth.*** I have found this to be most of the time. People are upset because they have half of the truth. In our society, there is an even greater tendency to rush to judgment based on incomplete information.

4. ***The presenting issue is rarely the real issue.*** It is always wise to hear a matter out because normally what most people are mad about is not really the real problem. Rather than reacting to what your critics say, Mike states, try to get to the root issue.

5. ***Sometimes critics can be turned.*** If you listen to people initially without being hostile toward their complaint, and rather than painting them as "demons," you may be surprised at the outcome.

Mike says these lessons are simple, but applying them isn't easy. He says, criticism will always sting. Be prepared for your critics, so that they don't stop the work that you have been called to do.

Never let anyone's criticism stop you from fulfilling your calling in life. If you do, you will go to your grave with the "music" inside of you.

Every jungle has predators. And if you are going to survive, it will require that you know your own proclivities and preferences, your default settings and disciplines.

Recommended Books to Read

Instinct by T. D. Jakes

The Heart of Business by Raymond H. Harris

Where Purpose Is Not Known, Abuse Is Inevitable

--Dr. Myles Munroe--

D r. Myles Munroe was one of the most incredible and powerful thought leaders in the 21st century. When he passed during the writing of this book, I felt impressed in my spirit to make this book a legacy for him and those who died in the plane crash on November 9, 2014, in the Bahamas.

Dr. Myles Munroe's teachings, writings and influence will live on in the hearts of those who have been exposed to him. So I am thrilled that God spoke to my heart to close this book out with a wealth wisdom principle from him. But in case you have never heard of Dr. Munroe, I want to share his biography with you.

Dr. Myles Munroe was an internationally renowned author, lecturer, teacher, life coach, government consultant, and leadership mentor. He spent the last thirty years traveling the world and training leaders in business, education, government, and religion. He delivered his message on personal and professional development to more than 500,000 people yearly and millions through his Media program.

Dr. Munroe was a multi-gifted, international motivational speaker, best-selling author, and business consultant to governments, Fortune 500 Companies, and corporations, addressing the critical issues that affect every aspect of human, professional, leadership, social, and spiritual development. Plus, he wrote over 38 books.

Dr. Munroe was invited to over 80 nations as an ambassador of his nation; the Bahamas to address government bodies, business leaders, universities, and religious organizations as well. Dr. Munroe was his nation's youngest recipient of the Queen's Birthday Honors of the Order of The British Empire (OBE) Award 1998, which was bestowed on him by Her Majesty Queen Elizabeth of England for his spiritual and social contributions to the national development of the Bahamas. He has also been honored by the government of the Bahamas with the Silver Jubilee Award (SJA) for providing 25 years of outstanding service to the Bahamas in the category of spiritual, social and religious development.

Taken from https://mylesmunroeinternational.com/about-us/

As you can see by Dr. Munroe's biography, he was an extraordinary, incredible leader. In fact, his name was a legend among the clergy and government communities. One of the greatest quotes he was known for was, ***"Where purpose is not known, abuse is inevitable."*** He said, when we don't know the purpose of a thing, there will always be a level of abuse. And it is the same when we don't know our purpose in life.

When we don't know what we are called to do in life, we will live a substandard life that is inferior to God's purpose for us. How many people have you heard about that have gone to college and got a degree in a certain major, but it really was not their passion? Perhaps, someone told them this career or that career will allow them to live comfortably, only to find out in the end, it was not what they were called or purposed to do. So instead of living comfortably, they are frustrated.

Perhaps this is you. You have spent many years doing something you were not happy doing or that did not fulfill you. You are working a job that you do not like and you feel like you are being abused. Guess what, you probably are. When you are not properly aligned with your purpose or innate calling, your gift will be abused.

However, I have good news for you. You can start today and make a decision to change your situation. The sooner you come in alignment with your purpose, the sooner the things that you need to fulfill your purpose will begin to come into your equation. This happens to me repeatedly.

When I need something in my business and I don't know anyone who can assist me, I press in really hard into prayer meditating on my need, so that it can be brought into my equation. If God knows everything, then He knows people in every arena. As long as what I ask for is definitely about fulfilling my destiny and purpose in life, then I know it is only a matter of time before God will provide what I need.

You were ordained to be great before you were born (Jeremiah 1:4). Don't allow what you were called to do in this earth be abandoned or abused. Your gift is to be used to bless the world. Your gift is to be used to bless your life and your family. Find out what God has called you to do in this earth and go after it with all your heart. Otherwise, you will be living a substandard life for the rest of your life. Why abuse a precious jewel like you?

**Here are some more quotes by Dr. Myles Munroe.
Be blessed by them.**

*"The greatest tragedy in life is not death,
but a life without a purpose."*

*"You must decide if you are going
to rob the world or bless it with the rich,
valuable, potent, untapped resources
locked away within you."*

"People generally fall into one of three groups: the few who make things happen, the many who watch things happen, and the overwhelming majority who have no notion of what happens. Every person is either a creator of fact or a creature of circumstance. He either puts color into his environment, or, like a chameleon, takes color from his environment."

"One of the greatest tragedies in life is to watch potential die untapped."

"...success is not a comparison of what we have done with what others have done."

Wealth Nugget From This Chapter

*When we don't know
what we are called to do in life,
we will live a substandard life
inferior to what God had
purposed for us.*

Recommended Books to Read

Maximizing Your Potential by Dr. Myles Munroe

Consciously Wealthy by Richard Harper

Made in the USA
Charleston, SC
11 January 2016